EYE

BENDERS

EYE

BENDERS

CLIVE GIFFORD

Consultant **Professor Anil Seth**

BARRON'S

First edition for the United States, its territories and
possessions, and Canada published in 2014 by
Barron's Educational Series, Inc.

Copyright © Ivy Press Limited 2013

This book was conceived, designed & produced by

Ivy Press

210 High Street

Lewes

East Sussex BN7 2NS

United Kingdom

www.ivypress.co.uk

All inquiries should be addressed to:
Barron's Educational Series, Inc.
250 Wireless Boulevard, Hauppauge, New York 11788
www.barronseduc.com

ISBN: 978-1-4380-0366-5

Ivy Press

CREATIVE DIRECTOR	Peter Bridgewater
COMMISSIONING EDITOR	Georgia Amson-Bradshaw
MANAGING EDITOR	Hazel Songhurst
PROJECT EDITOR	Claire Saunders
CONSULTANT	Professor Anil Seth
ART DIRECTOR	Kim Hankinson
DESIGNERS	Joanna Clinch
	& Kevin Knight

Library of Congress Control No. 2013943177

Product conforms to all applicable CPSC and CPSIA 2008
standards. No lead or phthalate hazards.

Manufactured by: Lion Productions, China
Date of manufacture: November 2013

9 8 7 6 5 4 3 2 1

CONTENTS

IS SEEING REALLY BELIEVING?

Lucky you! As a human being you have been equipped with terrific eyesight (either naturally or corrected with glasses, contact lenses, or laser surgery) that feeds incredibly detailed visual information to your enormously powerful brain. Your amazing eyes and ever-so-clever brain work together to form a powerful vision system. It allows you to view and make sense of the world around you, to recognize a vast range of shapes, colors, and objects, to spot tiny details or gawk at amazing wide-screen, panoramic scenes. It also allows you to read these very words.

But not all is perfect. Your eyes and brain are not foolproof and can be tricked in different ways by a wide range of optical illusions. This book, jam-pack with imagery trickery—from street art that plays with perspective, to color, depth, and geometrical illusions—reveals how our brains and eyes work. Along the way, you'll learn about blind spots, retinal rods and cones, your vision processing centers, and the way your brain merges your two eyes' views into one picture. You could say it's all pretty eye-mazing! Remember, certain illusions work better for some people than others, so don't worry if you can't see the effects in all of them.

Here's just a taste of some of the different types of illusions you'll find in this book.

FISH OUT OF WATER

Can you get the fish into the bowl? Here's a clue—start off by staring hard at the fish for 45 seconds. For more illusions like this, turn to pages 24 and 25.

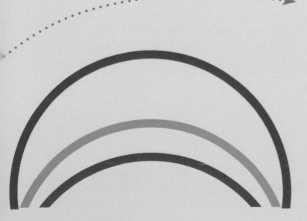

CUBE COUNT

What's the most number of cubes you can see in this image? Are you sure? Turn the book 90 degrees and see how many you can count now. Turn to page 52 for more illusions like this.

COLOR CONFUSION

How many different colors do you see on this cube created by neuroscientist R. Beau Lotto? You'll be amazed at the answer. There are more color illusions on pages 28 to 31.

Turn to page 63 for the answers.

ARC TEASE

Which of these arcs comes from the biggest circle? Easy, isn't it? There are more size illusions like this on pages 32 to 35.

SPIRAL OR CIRCLES?

Is this picture made up of a spiral or circles? Are you sure? Look again! The Café Wall Illusion on page 39 works in a similar way.

SAY HELLO TO YOUR BRAIN

This is where it all happens, where all your thoughts, plans, dreams, and actions occur. Your brain controls all the different parts of your body, allows your senses to experience the outside world, and stores all of your memories. Pretty impressive for something weighing less than 5 pounds (2 kilograms) and about the size of a small cauliflower.

Protected by the skull, which forms a bony crash helmet, the outer part of your brain is called the cerebral cortex and is split into left and right halves, or hemispheres. The halves are connected by a bundle of approximately 250 million nerve fibers. The entire brain is connected to the rest of the nervous system (see page 10) via the brain stem and spinal cord. Each half of the cerebral cortex of your brain is split into a number of parts, called lobes, all of which are responsible for different tasks. With so much going on in your brain, it's no surprise that it uses a lot of your body's energy — about one-fifth, in fact.

FRONTAL LOBE

This lobe is responsible for your deeper thinking, such as how you learn skills and facts and how you plan steps toward achieving a goal. It is also involved in helping you make deliberate movements of your muscles and body.

TEMPORAL LOBE

Found low down on each side of the brain, these regions are involved in making memories and helping you recognize particular objects.

BRAIN STEM

The brain stem connects the brain to the spinal cord (see page 11). It controls the things that happen automatically in your body without you thinking about them, such as digesting food, maintaining your heart rate, and breathing.

CEREBELLUM

The cerebellum organizes the signals sent out to muscles so that your movements are smooth and accurate. It also helps you keep your balance, and recognize spaces and distances to and from objects.

PARIETAL LOBES

These lobes are busy, busy, busy. They tell you what you feel with your fingertips, alert your body when you feel pain or hot or cold temperatures, and are also involved in controlling tasks such as writing and drawing.

OCCIPITAL LOBES

Located at the back of your brain, these lobes process all the signals sent from your eyes through the optical nerve to give you your sense of sight. They also allow you to recognize shapes and colors.

NERVE NETWORK

To work well, your brain needs vast amounts of information sent to it from every part of your body. This lets your brain know how your body is functioning and also gives it data about the outside world. Your nervous system is your body's information highway. It's made up of millions of nerve cells called neurons, bundled into fibers that extend throughout your body.

Nerve signals are tiny electrical impulses. These make a one-way trip along nerve fibers either to or from the brain. Sensory nerves carry signals to your brain from your eyes, ears, skin, and other parts of your body. Signals also travel the other way along motor nerves from your brain to your muscles, instructing them to relax or contract to move a body part.

PERIPHERAL NERVES

Signals travel from a part of your body along nerve fibers in the peripheral nervous system to the spinal cord.

BRAIN

Your brain, together with your spinal cord, forms your central nervous system. The brain has a phenomenally large job to deal with the millions of nerve signals it receives.

OPTIC NERVE

Your eyes generate so many signals, millions every second, that each eye has its own dedicated information highway, the optic nerve.

SPINAL CORD

This cord of nerve tissue runs through your spine. It's nearly 17.5 inches (45 centimeters) long in an adult and weighs 1–1.5 ounces (35–40 grams—the weight of a large strawberry), yet it carries vast numbers of signals to and from the brain, which it joins at the brain stem.

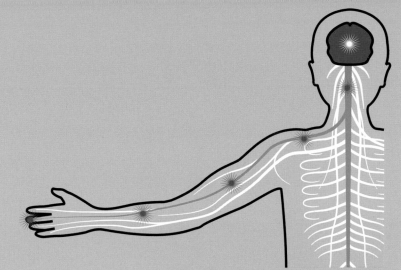

A NERVOUS JOURNEY

When you touch a sharp object, pain receptors in your skin send signals along sensory nerves in your finger. These signals travel along the nerve fibers at speeds of up to nearly 400 feet (120 meters) per second—nearly 270 miles (430 kilometers) per hour. Your brain may send back an instant response along motor nerves to your finger muscles, telling them to move away from the source of pain.

PROPRIOCEPTION: FEEL THE FORCE

Your body is constantly sending information through your nervous system to keep track of all your individual parts. If it didn't, your body parts wouldn't work very well together and you'd be an uncoordinated mess. This sense is called proprioception.

To see it in action, place your left arm above your head, close your eyes, and try to touch your nose with your right index finger and then your left thumb with your right index finger. Despite no vision to guide you, your finger will find its targets. This is because your nervous system is constantly updating your brain on the position of your nose, arms, and fingers.

11

EYE, EYE

Your eyes sit in bony sockets in your skull. They are protected upfront with eyelashes, eyelids, and tear ducts that give the front of your eye a good windshield wash with tears every few seconds when you blink. This salty solution is supplied by tear glands about the size of an almond. The front of your eye has a tough, thin, see-through coating called the cornea for added protection.

Light enters the front of the eye through the cornea and a small dark hole called the pupil. It then travels through the clear lens, which focuses the light so that it hits a layer at the back of the eye called the retina. There, approximately 120–130 million special cells called rods and cones detect light and convert it into tiny electrical signals. After some more processing, these are sent down the optic nerve to the brain.

CORNEA

This curved, see-through covering at the front of the eye protects the iris and pupil and helps focus light.

PUPIL

The black hole in the center of your eye, through which light enters.

IRIS

The colored part of the eye, usually gray, green, blue, or brown. Tiny muscles inside the iris control how much light enters the eye by changing the size of the pupil.

LENS

This transparent, flattened sphere focuses light onto the back of the eye. Ciliary muscles hold it in place.

SCLERA

The tough, outer coating of most of your eyeball. This is the part you see when you look at the whites of someone's eyes.

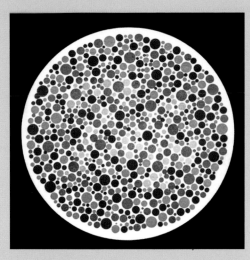

COLOR BLINDNESS

Some people have a greater or lesser degree of color blindness, with some or all of their cone cells not functioning as well as they could. Total color blindness is rare and means someone cannot see in color at all. The more common form of color blindness is when people struggle to tell the difference between red and green. Take a look at this test for color blindness, the Ishihara Test. What can you see? Turn to page 63 for the answer.

RETINA

Located at the back of the eye, the retina is packed with millions of photoreceptors—cells known as rods and cones, which react to specific wavelengths of light and trigger nerve impulses. Rods are sensitive to lightness and darkness, shape, and movement, and they allow you to see in low-light conditions. Cones are sensitive to color and are much fewer in number—there are 16 or 17 rod cells for each cone.

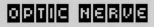

OPTIC NERVE

Each optic nerve is made up of about a million nerve fibers. These carry signals from your eyes to your brain.

VITREOUS HUMOR

This is no laughing matter. It's the colorless, jellylike filling that makes up about 80 percent of your eye and helps give it its shape.

THE LENS

Located just behind the pupil and iris, the lens is a crucial part of your vision system. It is convex (curves outward) both at its front and its rear. This shape means that light reaching the lens is bent as it travels through it. It is this bending that enables you to focus on an image or object you want to view.

Light likes to travel in straight lines, but as it reaches the eyes it is bent double. The curved cornea bends light toward the pupil in the center of your eye, which opens wider in low light to let more light in and narrows when the light is bright. Light entering the pupil is then bent again when it reaches the lens. To be focused — nice and clear and sharp — light from nearby sources needs more bending than light from farther away. So, the lens is squeezed or stretched to change shape, depending on what you are viewing.

UPSIDE DOWN

When you look at a scene or object, such as this bird, light is taken in by the eye. It is refracted (the fancy scientific word for "bent") by the lens so that the image is focused sharply on the retina at the back of the eye ... but upside down. Don't worry, this information is carried to the vision centers of your brain, which perceive them the right way up.

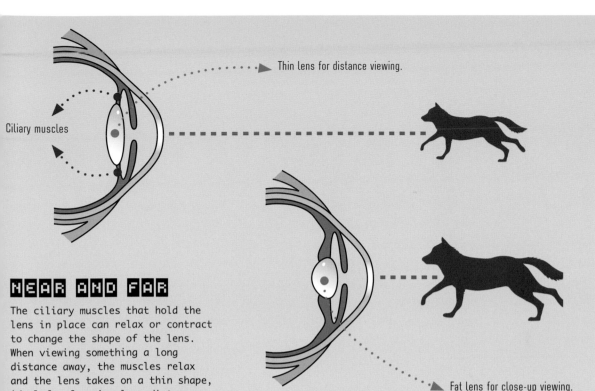

Thin lens for distance viewing.

Ciliary muscles

Fat lens for close-up viewing.

NEAR AND FAR

The ciliary muscles that hold the lens in place can relax or contract to change the shape of the lens. When viewing something a long distance away, the muscles relax and the lens takes on a thin shape, ideal for focusing long distance. When viewing something much closer, the muscles get shorter and the lens gets fatter and rounder to provide near vision.

MAKE A PINHOLE CAMERA

Making a pinhole camera can help you understand how your own eyes work. You'll need a cardboard potato chip tube or similar, some wax paper or other thin paper, a rubber band, and a compass. Cut out a circle of paper 1–2 inches [3–5 centimeters] wider than the tube and stretch it tight over the opening, holding it in place with the rubber band. Poke a small hole in the bottom of the tube with the compass. Stand in a dark room with the curtains closed and point the pinhole end of the tube past the curtains to look out at a bright object outside. You should see an image on the paper of the scene upside down.

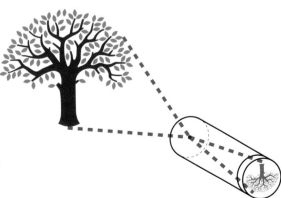

SCAN SCAM

Your eyes possess a powerful autofocus system, a little like a digital camera, but it can be a bit twitchy. Your eyes rarely stay completely still. Instead, they often make tiny, involuntary movements, which scientists call microsaccades, as they scan the scene in front of them. Your eyes also make frequent, small adjustments to their lenses to alter focus. Some illusions exploit these eye movements to create illusions that appear to change in size, appear closer, or actually move on the page. Some of these optical illusions are not completely understood yet by science, but that doesn't mean they're not a lot of fun.

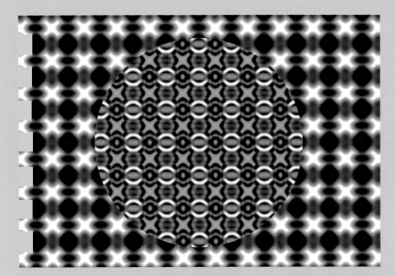

GROWS ON YOU

Focus on the image below and watch in amazement as the diamonds seem to grow. What's happening is that as your eyes focus on the diamonds, the background appears to fade away and the diamonds increase in size.

ARTIFICIAL DEPTH

The circle and the patterned background above are on the same piece of paper, but the blurring of the background helps trick your eyes and brain into believing that the circle is closer to your eyes than the background and so is floating above it. This is sometimes known as artificial depth.

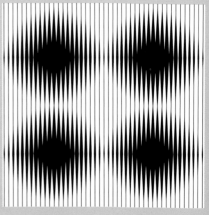

SWAYING LEAVES

These leaves are not moving, honest.
However, your brain is tricked by
the different angles of the leaves
and their light and dark edges to
believe that they are gently swaying
or flowing across the page.

ON THE MOVE

Take a long look at the image to
the right. See how, after a few
seconds, it starts moving, with
the center of the image collapsing
in on itself and the outer edges
seeming to move away from the
center. This motion illusion occurs
because your eyes are constantly
moving and scanning the scene.

IN A SPIN

There are many illusions that don't just make the image seem to sway or grow, but to actually turn or spin. These are motion illusions, just like those on pages 16 and 17, but the shading, coloring, and the shapes in the illusions here create a curved or circular movement, partly due to your eyes moving to take in the whole image. The difference between how much light the different colors give off in the patterns, called luminance, is also thought to play a part in the illusion.

The modern master of motion illusions like these is Japanese psychologist Professor Akiyoshi Kitaoka. After studying burrowing behavior in rats and looking at how macaque monkeys think, Kitaoka turned his attention to human vision. He then produced a stack of über-cool illusions, several of which have inspired the ones you see here.

If the illusion stops, rev it up again by rapidly scanning left and right across the image.

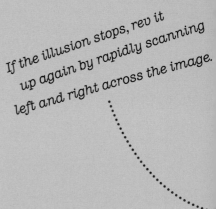

SPINNING SNAKES

One of Akiyoshi Kitaoka's most famous illusions, which has been copied by dozens of artists, was unveiled in 2003. It shows a large number of wheels or curled snakes in blue and yellow, like the ones shown here. If the whole image is scanned by your eyes, instead of you staring at one single point, all the wheels seem to turn slowly around.

IN A SPIN

This illusion was inspired by a creation of Israeli painter Isia Leviant in 1981 and still confuses people today. If you stare at the center of the image for a few seconds, you'll start to see parts of the black circles scintillate or twinkle. This is followed by light appearing to race around the circles.

TURNING CYLINDERS

In this awesome illusion, all there is on the page are a large number of blue ovals and circles, but your brain not only perceives them as forming the sides of three tubes or cylinders, it actually makes them rotate before your very eyes.

BLIND SPOT

Alert: Your retina isn't the perfect, all-seeing power-packed vision sensor you may have thought it was. In fact, part of it cannot see anything at all. The optic nerve passes through part of the retina as it joins the eye, and it is this gap — which is full of optic nerve and not photoreceptor cells (rods and cones) — that is called your blind spot. In reality, you rarely notice your blind spot in everyday situations, but some fun illusions play on this flaw in your eye.

French scientist Edme Mariotte was the first person to discover the blind spot in humans all the way back in 1660, when he dissected a human eye ... ugh! Intrigued, Mariotte experimented with his own vision to discover that all people have a blind spot in each eye about one millimeter wide. At the time, it was thought that this part of the retina, being closest to the optic nerve, would be the most sensitive to light.

It's not just humans who have blind spots. Nearly all animals have them, except cephalopods. Squid, octopus, and cuttlefish have their optic nerves behind their retina, so they don't have a blind spot. Lucky them.

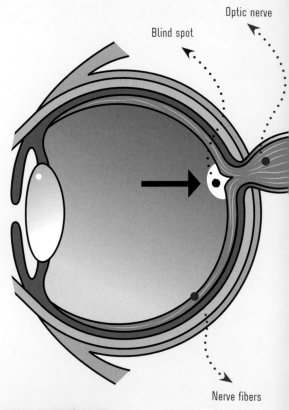

Optic nerve

Blind spot

Nerve fibers

NO SENSE

This diagram of the eye shows the optic nerve and the nerve fibers that run in front of the retina. These are nearly transparent, but light still has to travel through them to reach the retina. The blind spot occurs where the optic nerve passes through the retina.

1 2 3 4 5 6 7 8 9

SPOT YOUR BLIND SPOT

Here are two tests for you to find your very own blind spot. In both cases, keep your head still, close your right eye and use your left to view the numbers, starting with 1 and reading to the right. In the test above, you'll see the flower until you get to number 4 or so. Don't worry,

it makes a comeback when you reach number 7, or thereabout, having crossed your blind spot. In the picture below, a similar phenomenon occurs between numbers 4 and 7, with the gap in the purple line temporarily disappearing from view to make the line look complete.

1 2 3 4 5 6 7 8 9

MAKE AN ELEPHANT DISAPPEAR

Make an elephant disappear? No, we're not kidding! Holding the book at arm's length, close your left eye and with your right concentrate on the old-fashioned magician tapping his long wand. Now, bring the book slowly toward you. Abracadabra! For a short distance, the elephant vanishes from sight. Now, that's magic—or more accurately, your blind spot in action.

TWO IS BETTER THAN ONE

So far, we've mostly looked at one eye at a time. Now, let's see how they work as a pair. Your eyes are placed on the front of your head, giving you good vision ahead of you, but poorer vision to the sides. Some creatures such as birds, horses, and lizards have almost complete all-around vision because their eyes are on the sides of their heads, but they tend to have less overlapping vision from both eyes.

Your eyes are spaced about 2 inches (5 centimeters) apart. This small distance is a surprisingly big deal, as it means each eye sees a slightly different view of the world. The small difference in viewing is one of the major ways your brain calculates depth and the distances to objects. It does this by comparing the different angles of the objects it views. If you don't believe two eyes are better than one, try catching a ball or threading a needle with one eye closed and see how much harder it is.

FIELD OF VIEW

The "field of view" is how much of the world you can see at any one moment. The position of your eyes on your head gives you a wide field of view in front of you. A large portion of that view sees each eye's range overlap, providing you with a reasonably wide arc of binocular vision. This gives you good perception of depth and distances. The remainder of your vision—to your right and left sides—is with only one eye, so perception of depth in those fields is much poorer.

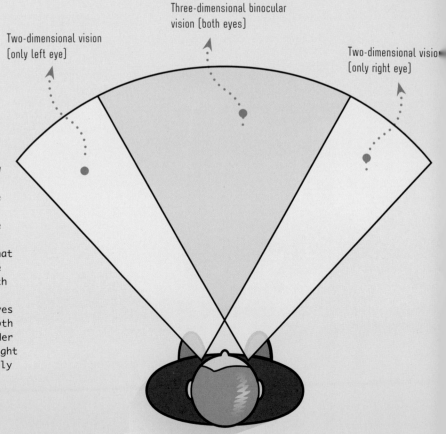

Two-dimensional vision (only left eye)

Three-dimensional binocular vision (both eyes)

Two-dimensional vision (only right eye)

PUT A HOLE IN YOUR HAND!

Your eyes each take in different views that your brain then combines to create a single complete image. Here's a cool experiment to demonstrate this.

Get a long cardboard tube, hold it up to your right eye, and look through the tube at a bright surface, such as a white or light-colored wall. Bring the palm of your other hand up in front of your face to the side of the tube and look at it with your left eye as you look through the tube with your right eye. What do you see?

Don't worry — that hole you see in your hand isn't really there. It's caused by your brain processing the view from each eye into a single image. Because most of the view from your right eye is of dark tube, your brain pays extra attention to the small circle of bright light and combines that with the clear image of your hand from your left eye. For an added twist, ask someone to wiggle their finger in the far end of the tube. Freaky!

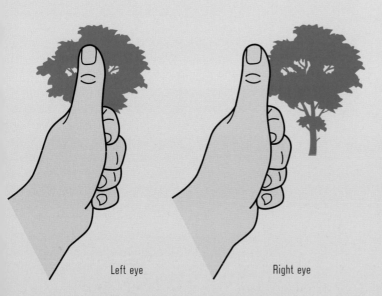

Left eye   Right eye

PARALLAX

Parallax is the difference in the apparent position of an object when viewed from two different locations, such as from your left eye and right eye. Your brain uses the parallax shift between your eyes as one way of measuring distances: the smaller the shift, the farther away an object tends to be. You can easily see parallax in action by closing one eye and sticking out your thumb to cover an object, such as a tree, flag, or distant building. Now close that eye and open the other and see how your thumb appears to have moved and changed position.

AFTER IMAGES

Afterimages are images that you continue to see after you've stopped looking directly at them. They are caused by the light sensitive cells in your retina, and the neurons (nerve cells) connected to them, tiring after looking at the same image for some time. The neurons take time to reset, ready for new images, and in this short space of time you get to see afterimages. They can create some pretty awesome effects.

You may not realize it, but you see afterimages every day. For example, if you are dazzled by bright car headlights (or some other strong white light source), as you look away you'll see a dark spot in your vision — the opposite of the light you were staring at. Some color afterimages occur because nerve cells handle pairs of colors — such as red and green, or blue and yellow. These are called opponent pathways. If one color is looked at for a while, when you look away, the nerve cells become more sensitive to the other color. So, after staring at a green stripe in the flag image below, you will probably see red when you look away.

STARS AND STRIPES

Place a sheet of blank white paper along the side of the book and then stare at the white dot in the center of this oddly colored image of the United States flag for 45 seconds. Now, look at the sheet of paper and you should see the flag in its correct colors.

TRUE COLORS

Stare at the dot in the center of this strangely colored view of Monument Valley (top image) for about 45 seconds. Then, quickly look down at the black-and-white version of the image beneath it and see what happens. You should see the scene in its correct colors, with orange rocks and a blue sky. As soon as you look away, the image will return to black and white.

FLOATING SKULL

Lock your gaze onto the X in the eye socket of this skull for at least 30 seconds. Now, look away at a light-colored surface and you should see a ghostly sight—a skull floating right before your very eyes. Creepy!

SHADES OF GRAY

Gray doesn't sound very interesting, but illusions in different shades of gray can be fascinating and surprising. Some, such as the Hermann Grid [see right], are caused by a phenomenon called lateral inhibition. When some of the neurons connected to the retina of your eyes send a signal on seeing an image, they stop or suppress their neighbors from sending signals. This is to help the brain and your whole vision system detect the edges of objects you're viewing. It also acts as a filter system that helps cut down the amount of information being processed by your brain.

In the illusions below, lateral inhibition has the effect of making blocks of the exact same shade appear more or less bright, depending on their surroundings. The lighter the surroundings, the darker they appear because of the amount of suppression from the neighboring neurons.

LIGHTER OR DARKER?

Look at the two small squares in the middle of the rectangle. Which square is the lighter? It appears to be the one on the right, but in fact both squares are the exact same shade. Your view is influenced by the lighter and darker shades that surround them.

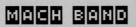

Spot the dots!

MACH BAND

Is each band of gray in this image the same shade throughout its width? It doesn't look like it, but it is. Lateral inhibition causes a band's left-hand edge—which borders the darker band—to look lighter and its edge that borders the lighter band to look darker.

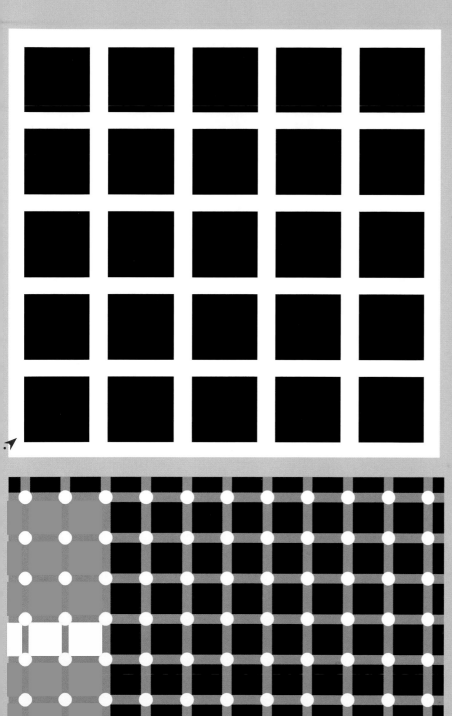

HERMANN GRID

This famous illusion was invented in 1870 and is named after its creator, the German scientist Ludimar Hermann. If you look at the grid of black squares, you'll see ghostly gray blobs appear where the white lines intersect each other. This illusion works best just to the sides of where you are focusing, because lateral inhibition occurs more in your peripheral vision, away from the center. If you stare directly at one intersection, the gray dot tends to disappear.

GOING DOTTY

This variation on the Hermann Grid already has circular white dots where the gray lines intersect. Look at one edge of the image and then stare at the center. You'll see dark and light dots appear and disappear at random on these intersections.

LIGHT & DARK

Our ability to see in color and in different shades of light and dark is a particularly handy aid for survival. It enables humans to pick out objects from a jumbled background that would be difficult to see in pure black and white. Color vision helped early peoples to identify colorful fruits and berries as food and to see dangerous threats, such as certain venomous snakes. However, the colors and shades of light and dark we think we see can be difficult for our brains to always identify correctly.

Although colors are registered by the cones in your retina, your brain sometimes processes them differently, according to other elements in the scene. For example, a color may appear lighter than it really is if it is surrounded by a background that is darker. Your brain can also be influenced by what it perceives as objects casting shadows over a scene; the two illusions on the opposite page show examples of this.

Are the small purple squares exactly the same shade as each other?

BRIGHTER AND LIGHTER

Look at the pair of squares with orange centers just above. Which of the orange squares seems a lighter shade? You'll probably answer the left one on the red background, but in fact they're both exactly the same shade. The same goes for the purple squares in the top image. When placed on a darker colored background, a colored area can appear clearer and brighter. This effect is called simultaneous brightness contrast.

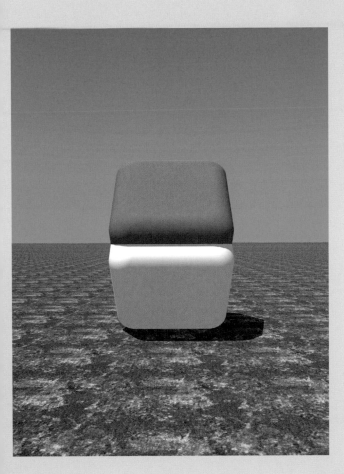

LOTTO CUBE

R. Beau Lotto is a neuroscientist who founded the Lotto Lab to investigate how our brains perceive things. This amazing illusion from the Lotto Lab features a cube whose white and gray edges convince your brain that the faces of the cube are quite different colors, with the "white" face merely in shadow. In fact, they are precisely the same shade of gray.

ADELSON CHECKERBOARD

This famous illusion was devised by Edward H. Adelson in 1995. Which of the two labeled squares is the darkest? If you answer A, like everyone does, you will be stunned to learn that you're WRONG! The two squares are actually the exact same shade. Look again. It still doesn't seem correct, does it? If you want proof, turn to page 63.

COLOR PUZZLERS

As we've seen, our brain doesn't always get things right when it comes to color and shades of light and dark. We don't view a single color in isolation. We view it as part of a scene where other colors are present. Sometimes, neighboring colors can influence the color the brain thinks it is seeing.

Below is an illusion that will scramble your brain. Look at the two squares indicated by the arrows and name their colors. In the left image, the bottom corner square is blue-green and in the right image, the top corner square is a pinkish hue ... or is it?

The amazing truth is that the two squares are both the same shade of the same color — gray. What's happening is that your brain is making assumptions about the light reflected from the image and is influenced by the colors around it. Other illusions, such as the red cross image (top right) and the Munker-White Illusion (bottom right), also use the presence of other colors nearby to trick your brain.

GURNEY ILLUSION

This astonishing illusion is by New York-based artist James Gurney. Look at the two squares indicated by the arrows in each picture. Then place pieces of paper over the image so that you can see only those two squares. What color do they look now?

COLOR CROSS

This X shape appears to be made up of small red and pink squares. In fact, the whole X and all of its squares are the same color. When the squares next to them are green, the squares look red, but when the neighboring squares are white, the red squares appear pink.

This X is made up of red and pink squares ... or is it?

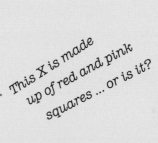

MUNKER-WHITE ILLUSION

Believe it or not, the two squares at the top are the exact same shade of red, and the two at the bottom are the same shade of green. The proximity of bright yellow bars surrounding and crossing the two left-hand squares tricks the brain into registering the squares as lighter than they really are.

BRAIN KNOWS BEST

Most of the time, your brain is working overtime. It is dealing with many, many different inputs from your senses, which send back millions of individual nerve signals every minute. To cope, your brain makes some assumptions and comparisons based on your memory and experience. Scientists don't completely understand how it manages to do this, but they do know it can sometimes get it wrong and be tricked into thinking that one thing is another.

Here are three sets of images that your brain makes mistakes in processing. The Two Tables Illusion was developed by Stanford University psychologist Professor Roger N. Shepard, in the 1990s, while the Jastrow Illusion is 100 years older. Both show how your brain makes a size comparison that it gets wrong in different ways.

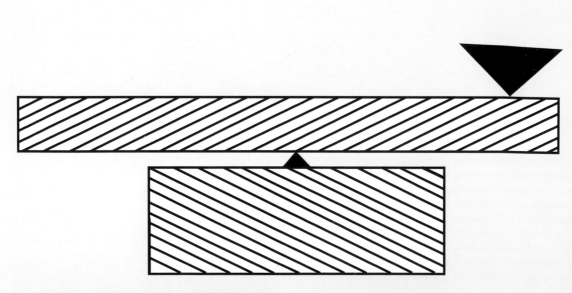

A QUESTION OF BALANCE

The simple shaded seesaw or balance below is tilted down on the right-hand side by the triangular weight resting on top of it ... Right? Wrong! The balance is totally, utterly level. The illusion is created partly through the diagonal line pattern and partly by the brain assuming that a weight on one side of a seesaw pushes that side down and the other side up.

TWO TABLES ILLUSION

Which table is longer? It looks pretty obvious, doesn't it? However, it's actually not as obvious as you think. Your brain sees the table on the left as stretching into the distance and assumes it is a lot longer. Get a ruler and measure both of the tables' long sides to get the answer.

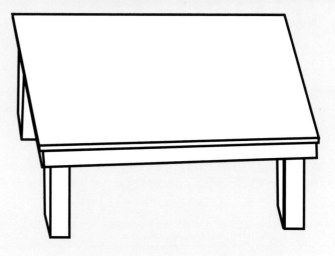

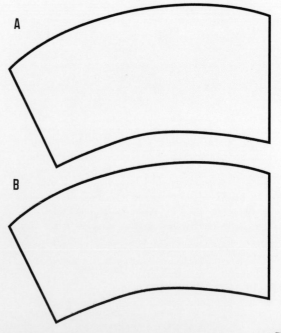

A

B

JASTROW ILLUSION

Is Shape B longer than Shape A? You have five seconds to decide. Quick! We guess that you'll say yes—but the answer is no. They're both the same size.

Cover Shape A with a piece of paper and use a piece of string to measure the top and bottom edges of Shape B. You'll find the top is longer than the bottom. Your eye and brain assess the size of the two shapes by comparing the two edges nearest to each other—the shorter, bottom edge of Shape A with the longer, top edge of Shape B.

SIZE SURPRISE

Your vision system is overloaded with tasks to do every minute of the day. Among them is figuring out the size of objects your eyes are viewing. You might think that this is simple; the bigger an item appears on the retina of your eye, the bigger it must be, but that doesn't allow for how far away the object is. After all, a single baked bean held up close to your eye dwarfs a 250-foot (76-meter) plane seen high in the sky.

Human vision systems have to make judgments about size, taking into account the object and its distance away, other objects around it, and any knowledge that your brain might have previously stored about that type of object. Sometimes, your eyes and brain will compare sizes between objects being viewed, but size comparisons can be influenced and distorted by illusions due to the closeness of other objects in the scene.

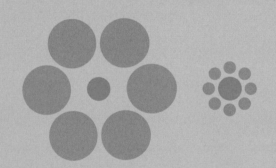

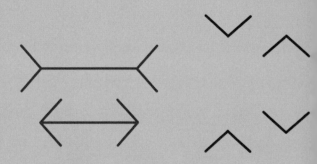

EBBINGHAUS ILLUSION

Take a quick glance at these two patterns of blue and orange circles. Which orange circle is the larger of the two? The one on the right, surely? Nope! They are both the same size. This is known as the Ebbinghaus Illusion and demonstrates how our sense of size can be influenced by the scale of surrounding objects.

MÜLLER-LYER ILLUSION

Look at the two red lines with arrows on the ends. Which line appears longest—the top or bottom one? Bet you said the top one. Although the two lines are the exact same length, the outward facing arrows on the top line trick our brain into thinking the line between them is longer. This is called the Müller-Lyer Illusion and it even works if you remove the actual line—as you can see if you look at the two sets of blue arrowheads. At first glance, there looks to be more space between the left pair, but get out a ruler and you'll see the distance is actually the same.

Is this arch taller than it is wide?

TOP HAT TRICK

This old-fashioned gentleman looks very smart in his top hat, but answer this question: Is the hat taller than it is wide? Most people would answer "yes," but the surprise is that the hat is as wide as it is tall. Many people fall for this illusion, because their brain overestimates the height of a vertical line when it joins with a horizontal line, making the horizontal line appear shorter than it really is. This phenomenon is not completely understood.

ST. LOUIS GATEWAY

Designed by architect Eero Saarinen, the St. Louis Gateway is a giant arch on the banks of the Mississippi River. It looks far taller than it is wide, doesn't it? But it's actually 630 feet (192 meters) wide and 630 feet (192 meters) tall—a real-life example of the Top Hat Illusion.

IN PERSPECTIVE

Your vision has to interpret a three-dimensional world, and it uses certain cues or rules to make sense of the distances and the sizes of objects. For example, when you are viewing two objects that your brain believes are the same, your vision system assumes that the larger one is closer.

"Linear" means straight line, and linear perspective is when parallel lines appear to come together, or converge, as they travel away from you and head off into the distance. These lines look like they meet at a point on the horizon known as the vanishing point. If there are two objects, and one of them is much closer to the vanishing point than the other, your vision tends to decide that that object is farther away.

Many centuries ago, artists didn't know about the rules of perspective, so their paintings appeared flat and lacking in depth. Linear perspective allows artists and designers to create scenes on a two-dimensional medium, such as paper, that look as if they are in three dimensions. It also allows some pretty nifty illusions to be created that trick you into misjudging the size of objects.

PONZO ILLUSION

Look at the two red bars lying across the railroad tracks. Which is bigger? The answer is neither. They're both the same size, but your brain's understanding of perspective and the narrowing railroad tracks makes the bar that is farther in the distance appear larger. This effect is called the Ponzo Illusion.

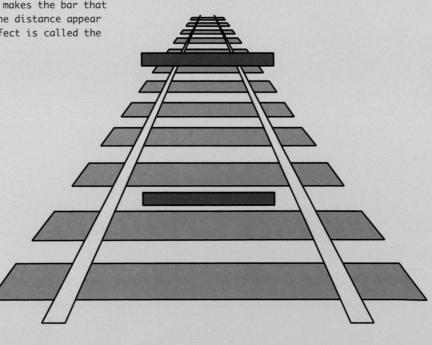

Look at this image by Professor Roger N. Shepard of a big monster chasing a smaller one. There's just one thing ... the two monsters are precisely the same size. This is a variation of the Ponzo Illusion using a tunnel instead of railroad tracks to give the illusion of depth. The rear monster appears to loom larger due to it being much closer to the vanishing point.

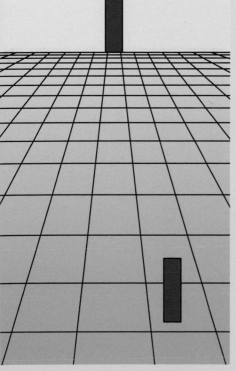

BLOCK BUSTERS

By now, you've probably guessed that these two blocks—just like the railroad track bars and the monsters—are identical in size, but at first glance they do look different. The rectangle on the horizon appears much farther away to your brain, which concludes that to appear that size at that distance, it must be larger.

STRAIGHT LINES

When is a straight line not a straight line? When your brain tells you it's not, that's when. A series of illusions have been found to trick your sense of vision into thinking a line or geometric object, such as a square or rectangle, is not quite what it should be. These illusions use surrounding colors, objects, or background patterns to trick you. Sneaky!

When you try to judge the straightness of a line, the size of an angle, or whether two lines on an image run parallel to one another, your brain can be influenced by other parts of the image. In trying to make sense of the images your eyes are taking in, your brain can be very easily fooled by backgrounds, the presence of other objects, and your brain's experience of perspective.

HERING ILLUSION

Take a look at the two bulging red lines in the image below. Use a ruler to measure the gap between them, and you'll see that there's no actual bulge—the lines are perfectly straight and run parallel. The radiating black lines create a sense of perspective heading off to a vanishing point in the middle that tricks your brain.

These bulging red lines aren't quite as they seem ...

ORBISON ILLUSION

This is called the Orbison Illusion and it shows squares on a background of concentric (one inside another) circles. The circles make the sides of some squares seem to bend inward, while the sides of other squares bend outward.

CAFÉ WALL ILLUSION

This famous illusion gets its name from the patterned tiles of a café in Bristol, England, which were "discovered" by Steve Simpson and investigated by psychologist Richard Gregory back in the 1970s. The series of tiled strips may appear crooked but, in fact, they run perfectly straight and parallel to each other.

ROOM WITH A VIEW

Your experiences in the past are held in your memory, which your brain uses to build up ways of recognizing objects. Your brain also relies on clues from the environment to estimate the size and distance of objects. When these clues are scrambled, distorted, or played with, interesting illusions can be created, including this pair, which are both based on altering the angles and perspective of something your memory is very familiar with — a room.

The Ames Room (see opposite page) was first thought up by American optician and scientist Adelbert Ames Jr., in 1934. When the Ames Room is viewed from the outside through a peephole, your brain decides it is seeing a regular rectangular room. Inside, two people stand in the two far corners. They both appear the same distance away from you, but one person seems tiny while the other looks like a giant. What can seem even more astonishing is that if the "giant" walks over to the smaller person, the giant suddenly shrinks in size.

The core of this illusion is simply a distorted-shaped room that is trapezoid in shape, not rectangular, so that the "small" person stands much farther back from you. The walls are slanted and the ceiling slopes downward from left to right, so that the giant looms large and the other person seems dwarfed by the room.

BALANCING ACT?

Take a look at this scene above. The man appears to be balancing precariously on some stacked furniture. He cannot remain in that position for more than a few seconds, your brain tells you. The truth is he could stay there for hours ... because he is lying on his side, as are the chairs, table, and stool. The image has been rotated at an angle of 90 degrees so the floor appears to be a wall—a simple but effective trick.

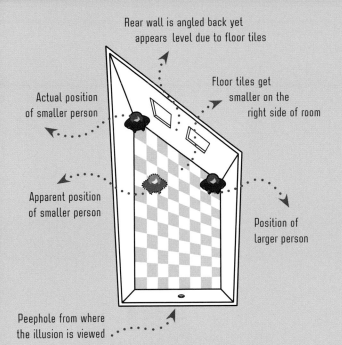

Rear wall is angled back yet appears level due to floor tiles

Floor tiles get smaller on the right side of room

Actual position of smaller person

Apparent position of smaller person

Position of larger person

Peephole from where the illusion is viewed

AMES ROOM

Look at the giant girl towering over the much smaller woman in the left-hand corner of the room below. The person who appears smaller is simply standing a lot farther away from you, but the room has been shaped to convince your brain they are the same distance from you. The floor squares are painted in different sizes to complete the illusion. The two people's feet are a similar size but the smaller orange tiles on the right-hand side of the room make the "giant's" foot appear much larger. The diagram on the left shows how this famous illusion works.

IN THE
DISTANCE

Your brain often strives to turn two separate scenes or two objects into one recognizable image. This leads to some interesting effects when illusions play with perspective, such as the Beuchet Chair Illusion (see opposite page), or distance.

For example, you've already seen how train tracks appear to get closer to each other as they recede into the distance. This phenomenon, linear perspective, applies not only when you look ahead but also when looking up, such as at tall buildings that rise vertically upward. If your brain sees two objects rising into the sky that do not get closer as they get farther away, it actually assumes that they are traveling away from each other, or diverging, and it may exaggerate the angle, as in the Leaning Tower illusion below.

A completely different type of distance illusion is the hybrid image. Hybrid images contain features from two separate images merged together. One set of features is best viewed close up, while the other is easier to see from a distance. So, as you move away from the image, it appears to change from one picture to another.

LEANING TOWERS

Take a look at these images of the famous Leaning Tower of Pisa. Can you see how the image on the right appears to lean more? In fact, the photos are identical. This illusion is based on one created by scientists at McGill University in Canada.

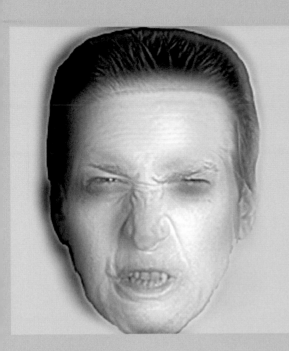

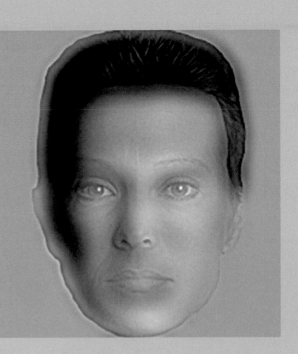

TWO FACED

That's one angry man on the left and one calm looking woman on the right—at least, it is when this hybrid image above is viewed close up. Now ask someone to hold the book up and step back 3–7 paces. Astoundingly, you'll see the faces switch expressions: the angry man becomes calm, and the calm woman becomes angry.

BEUCHET CHAIR

BEUCHET CHAIR

Invented by Frenchman Jean Beuchet in 1963, this trick chair plays with distance perspective and your brain's recognition of objects to convince you that you are viewing a tiny person sitting on a normal chair. In actuality, the sitter is a regular height, only sitting on a giant chair seat much farther away from the viewing point than the chair legs, which are a normal size. When the chair legs and chair seat are lined up, your brain perceives the two parts as one piece of furniture. Turn to page 63 to see precisely how this illusion is created.

43

FORCED PERSPECTIVE

Forced perspective is a technique found in photography, movies, and art. It uses an optical illusion to make an object appear closer or farther away or larger or smaller than it actually is. If you've seen a funny photo of someone holding a tiny human friend in the palm of their hand, you've already viewed an example.

In photography and film, forced perspective often relies on the careful lining up of two objects that are different distances from the camera. If the camera is focused correctly, this can give the impression that the objects are at a similar distance.

MAN MEAL

This man-eating lady is a classic example of forced perspective. The man who seems to be forming the lady's lunch stands a long distance back from the camera, so he appears much smaller in the photo. This technique exploits how your brain recognizes objects and their usual sizes to create a surprising or amusing image.

44

MOON MOVER

You've seen some heavy things carried by wheelbarrows but ... the moon? This simple illusion, created through careful lining up of the wheelbarrow and the moon, was created by French photographer Laurent Laveder.

RAINBOW ARTIST

Here's another fun example of forced perspective, this time showing someone apparently drawing a rainbow in the sky over the city of Honolulu in Hawaii.

NOW CREATE YOUR OWN

Why not try to make your own forced perspective image using your camera or cell phone? You'll need patience and a sharp eye to line up two objects in your viewfinder. To create an amusing effect, look for contrast between the two objects, such as a large landmark in the distance and a friend much closer to the camera. Take plenty of shots, if possible focusing on, or a short distance beyond, the closest object, and review your work to get the best possible picture.

If you're stumped for ideas, try one of the following:

▶ One person appearing to step on a tiny person.

▶ Holding or pushing a large landmark in the distance.

▶ A person in the distance balancing on an unlikely object nearby.

▶ A small pet appearing giant in size compared to people in the distance.

FILLING IN THE GAPS

As you saw when learning about the blind spot, your brain doesn't always get the complete picture, but that doesn't stop it from filling in the information it's missing. Sometimes, it does this by making assumptions, basing what it thinks it sees on its experience and what it calculates will probably be present. This can lead to some fascinating phenomena.

When faced with a grouping of different shapes or objects, your brain often considers them as a single scene and attempts to organize them into a pattern or order that it can understand and recognize. "Subjective contours," also known as "illusory contours," are where your brain fills in the gaps and "places" an edge or object on a scene when there is actually no change in color, brightness, or texture. This often occurs when your vision system sees an unusual shape and explains it as one shape overlapping another.

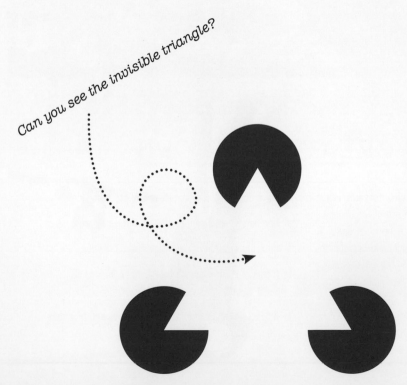

Can you see the invisible triangle?

KANIZSA TRIANGLE

Look at the image on the left. What do you see? If you answer three circles covered by a triangle, you'd be far from alone. That's what nearly everyone sees. However, the triangle isn't actually present; it has no edges and is the same color as the background. The three circles with segments cut out to look like the arcade game character Pacman generate this subjective contour illusion.

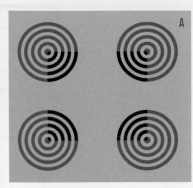

SUBJECTIVE CONTOURS

Here are four more subjective contour figures for you to look at. Your brain fills in the gaps between the circles in images (A) and (B) to form a square or a three-dimensional cube, respectively. Similarly, there is no actual sphere or ball in image (C) but your brain understands the pattern of cones as spikes sticking out of a ball. In image (D), an oval shape appears to float above the background of black horizontal lines, yet there is no actual oval. Your eyes tend to separate two sets of parallel lines, forming a border between them.

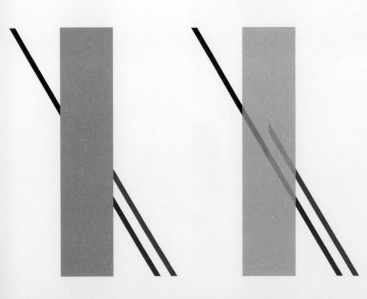

POGGENDORFF ILLUSION

This illusion was discovered in 1860 and scientists today still debate why it happens. Cover the right-hand image with a piece of paper and look down at the black slanted line in the left-hand image. Does it appear to continue on to the blue or the red line? Most people pick blue but, as the right-hand image shows, it actually joins up with the red line. A further mystery is provided if you move the book to your side and glance at the image out of the corner of your eyes. Then, the red and black lines do seem to line up.

3D TRICKERY

For centuries, artists have used their understanding of perspective and shading to make a flat surface look like a three-dimensional one. Some artists, both in the past and present, create exciting and puzzling illusions by taking these techniques to extremes.

"Trompe l'oeil" are artworks that deceive the eye by appearing to show realistic three-dimensional scenes or objects on flat surfaces. Sometimes these effects are produced inside a building to make it appear that it possesses pillars, extra doors, curved domes, or other architectural features where there is really just a flat surface.

Not a real dome

DOME ALONE

This domed ceiling is found at Saint Ignatius church in Rome and is a fake. It's an optical illusion painted by Andrea Pozzo between 1685 and 1697. Through clever use of light and shade, Pozzo was able to make the slightly curved ceiling of the church look like a large real-life dome.

Today, artists such as Julian Beever, Joe Hill, Kurt Wenner, Edgar Müller, and Tracy Lee Stum produce astonishing artworks on the outsides of buildings or on the sidewalks of city streets. These trick the brain into thinking it is seeing a surprising view inside a building or looking down a steep hole or cliff, when all the audience is doing is staring at flat sidewalks or streets.

DON'T TRIP!

This street illusion by British artist Joe Hill was made in Madrid, Spain, in 2012 for the movie release of "The Dark Knight Rises." When viewed from certain angles, its forced perspective gives a convincing illusion of depth and a dizzying drop, even though it is actually painted on a flat area.

FALLING DOWN

Celebrated artist Julian Beever produced this awesome optical illusion on a street in the Austrian city of Vienna. Our brain tells us the falling man is obviously a drawing made of chalk, but it takes a lot longer for our brain to realize that all the scaffolding and planks of wood, even the ones the real man at the top of the image is kneeling on, are just chalk art on a two-dimensional flat section of pavement.

AMBIGUOUS IMAGES

Did you know some images can offer you twice the value of others? These ambiguous (also known as bistable) images are drawn or painted in such a way as to give your vision system a choice of things to believe it is seeing. Although nothing changes on the page, there is more than one way for your vision system to interpret what is before your eyes.

When you look at an ambiguous image, there's every chance that your brain will lock onto one interpretation of the image at first. Aha, that's a man on a bicycle, it might think, for example, but as signals keep reaching your vision system, your brain will probably work out what else the image might be. Both explanations are as probable or valid as each other, so your brain can never truly decide which is correct and flips between the two. That's the fun of ambiguous images!

Find the hidden face!

AMBIGUOUS ART

Oleg Shuplyak is a talented artist from the Ukraine. He is best known for creating paintings that contain more than one image. Take a look at this picture, called "Science and Religion." It's of a woman reading underneath an archway, with a hooded figure nearby and the countryside beyond ... or is it? Look a little closer and you should also be able to see the large face of an old man—the famous naturalist, Charles Darwin.

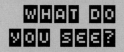

Here are four more ambiguous images. At first glance, you will probably identify them as one thing, but if you look at the images for a little longer, there's every chance you'll see an alternative interpretation. Write down what you think you can see in each image and check out the answers on page 63.

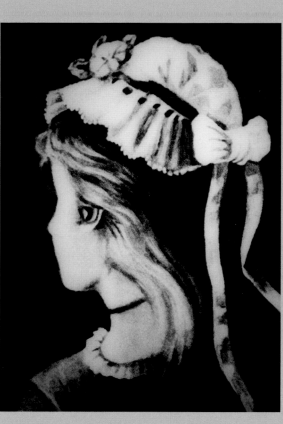

UPSIDE DOWN

The images your eyes see are focused on your retina upside down. Your brain then processes them to give you a right-way-up view. Sometimes your brain, in its haste to get things the right way around, can be tricked by carefully constructed drawings and illusions. It may also struggle when an image is not oriented in the way it expects.

One particular upside-down illusion (see opposite page, bottom) works with your brain's ability to spot and identify faces and facial features. Certain parts of your brain are dedicated to facial recognition and they're pretty good at it ... normally. Your brain works best with faces the right way up. When shown an upside-down face with parts of the face turned 180 degrees, your brain may recognize individual features of the face, such as the nose or mouth, but not whether or not they're the right way around. These images are called Thatcherized illusions. They get their name from Peter Thompson who first devised them in 1980, using a photo of former British Prime Minister Margaret Thatcher.

Can you move a glass off this tray?

MAGIC TRAY

There appear to be two glasses on this tray. How can you get one of them off the tray without touching it? Simple. Just turn the book upside down. This simple but mightily effective illusion was originally devised by scientist and writer Gianni A. Sarcone.

These two women, one old, one young, are the exact same image, just rotated 180 degrees. It turns out that these types of illusion have been around for centuries. In 2006, a 1,700-year-old ancient Roman mosaic was discovered in the town of Pomezia, 12 miles (20 kilometers) south of Rome, Italy; it depicted a young man when viewed from one direction and an old man when seen from the other.

THATCHERIZED FACES

Both of the above images appear to be the face of a young woman, only turned upside down. Now, turn the book upside down. The image on the edge of the page suddenly looks horribly freaky, doesn't it? That's because the eyes and mouth have been cut and pasted upside down on the face. Your brain identified the features as a mouth and eyes but didn't perceive that they were the wrong way up.

FACE FACTS

Have you ever seen the face of a celebrity on a piece of toast, or spotted a friend's face in a cloud? Maybe not, but chances are you have noticed shapes and marks in the natural world or on everyday items that appear to you as faces. There's even a technical term for it — pareidolia — which is the phenomenon of people's brains forming recognizable images from random markings and patterns.

Your brain is always on the lookout for patterns and order in the jumbled confusion of all the data your eyes send to it. Patterns can help your brain make sense of complicated scenes, and one element of this is your face recognition ability, which originates in the temporal lobes of your brain. Many scientists think that this is something people are born with as a survival aid, so that they can quickly separate family members from strangers, and friends from enemies. At times, your face recognition ability means you see a face where there really isn't one. In contrast, some people have a lack of face recognition ability, a condition known as prosopagnosia, or face blindness.

CLOCKING OFF

Look at the pictures below. They are simply the backs of two clocks, but which one is happy and which one looks downright miserable? You'll answer this in an instant, due to your brain's habit of arranging the random pattern of buttons, screws, and curved slots into the key parts of a face. And if you look to the right, you can't fail to see yet another face, this time on the grille of an entry phone and mail slot.

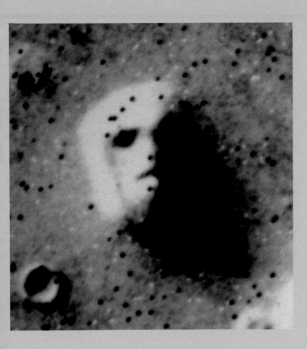

FACES EVERYWHERE

People see faces all over
the planet and beyond.
The Grey Man of Merrick
(below) is a famed chunk of
weathered rock in Scotland
that looks like an old man
from some angles. The image
on the left is a two-mile-
(three-kilometer-)long rock
formation from the surface
of Mars. It caused great
excitement when the image
was beamed back to Earth
from the Viking I space
probe in 1976.

IMPOSSIBLE IMAGES

In 1958, Lionel Penrose, a psychologist, and his son Roger, a mathematician, had an article called "Impossible Objects" published in a psychology journal. It introduced to the wider world simple yet curious drawings of images and figures that our brains struggle with. Impossible figures or objects have been perplexing people ever since.

When you view a two-dimensional picture on paper, your brain often interprets it as a three-dimensional figure, scene, or object, thanks to the artist drawing it in a certain way. Artists who produce impossible objects break some of the rules by making the drawing from different viewpoints and perspectives at the same time. They're just illustrations on the page, but your brain perceives them as having three dimensions and gets confused because they simply cannot be built in real-life.

To draw your own impossible shape, turn to page 59.

FAMOUS FIGURES

These three classic impossible figures are real brain benders. How can the struts form the frame of that cube on the left? Follow one beam of the triangle around and watch as it impossibly travels from being on the outside to being on the inside of the triangle. Count how many prongs the figure on the right has. Is it two or three?

PENROSE STAIRS

Look at any one of the figures on the move. They each appear to be climbing the steps of a toy brick staircase. All four staircases appear to be joined to one another and lead upward without getting any higher. How is that possible? Purely by your brain treating the image as a three-dimensional object when it is really a flat illustration on the page.

IMPOSSIBLE ELEPHANT

How many legs does this elephant appear to have in this famous puzzler from Professor Roger N. Shepard? It must be four, right? But look closely as you count and it starts to get confusing.

EXTREME SCENES

Some artists have taken impossible objects to the extreme, creating incredible scenes that challenge our brains. The most famous of these is the Dutch artist Maurits Cornelis (M. C.) Escher (1898–1972). Escher was fascinated by geometry and perspective in art and used these, along with careful positioning of light and shadows, to create impossible scenes, which inspired other artists to produce their own versions.

THE TERRACE

In David MacDonald's brain-bending 1999 artwork, "The Terrace," the paved area looks flat, yet a builder climbs a ladder to reach another part of it. Place your hand over the top or bottom half of the image and all looks well, but viewed all together it makes a perplexing picture.

RELATIVITY

In this reality-challenging engraving by M. C. Escher, "Relativity" (left), the normal laws of gravity don't seem to apply. Sixteen people are shown sitting or walking along staircases as if gravity is pulling on them in different directions. Turn the book 45 or 90 degrees and the scene changes.

MISSION: DRAW IMPOSSIBLE

It's easy to create your own impossible figure. First, draw six long lines parallel with each other and then give pairs of them pointed tops. Shade a little of the right-hand side of each column.

Next, place a piece of paper over almost all of the image, leaving only the ends of the lines visible at the bottom. Draw a curved line from line 1 to join the bottom of line 5. Do the same between lines 2 and 4. Then add the other two lines shown in red on the diagram.

Remove the paper and view your handiwork. You've created your own impossible image!

STEREOGRAMS

A stereogram is a flat, two-dimensional image that has been carefully prepared to produce a magical three-dimensional effect when viewed in the right way. Many stereograms are created by artists using computers, and some stereograms contain astonishing three-dimensional objects that appear hidden from view unless you look at them for a good, long time.

Seeing a stereogram can be tricky if you've never looked at one before, so be patient and take your time. When you're looking at the stereogram on the opposite page, stare at the image and try to let your eyes relax so you look through or past the image. Keep the page flat throughout and don't give up if you don't see the hidden image at first.

One tip is to bring the stereogram image up to your eyes until the page touches your nose. Your eyes cannot focus on the page and you automatically look behind the image. Keep your eyes from focusing on the page as you move it slowly away from you and the hidden image should come into view.

HIDING DEER

Here's an example of a stereogram (left) and its hidden picture, to give you an idea of what you're looking for in the stereogram on the opposite page. It's by supertalented Gene Levine of Color Stereo. On first inspection, the picture looks like a jumbled-up mess of color, but look a little closer and you can see it is made up of repeated patterns of scrubland. When people stare at this stereogram in full size, a large three-dimensional deer (below left) miraculously appears!

ICE IS NICE

Now, look at the right-hand page and shiver at this wintry scene by Gene Levine. Turn the book, lay the page flat, and stare through the stereogram to see what creatures are quite happy living there. Good luck!

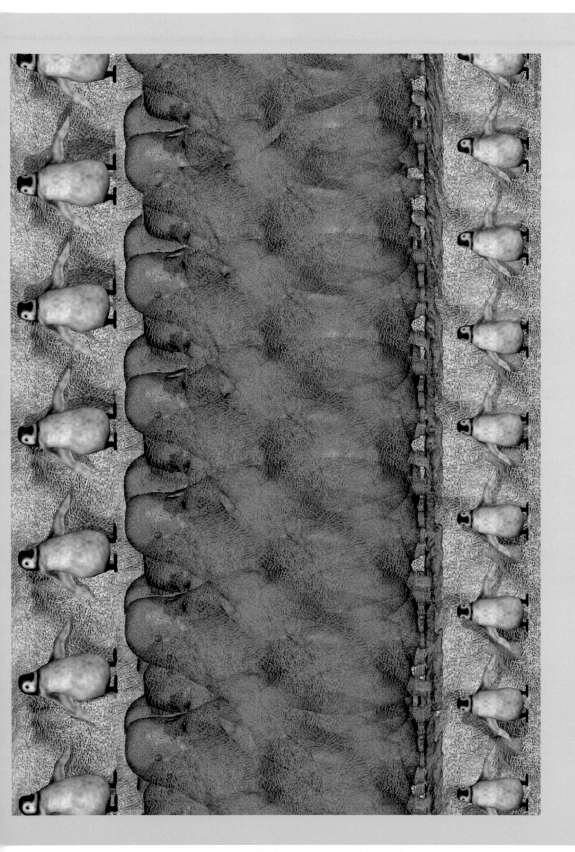

GLOSSARY

afterimage
A type of optical illusion where an image continues to appear in your vision after you have looked away.

ambiguous image
A type of optical illusion that has more than one image in it.

aperture
A hole or opening, such as the pupil in the eye, which lets light in.

binocular vision
Vision where both eyes are used at the same time, giving you good perception of distance and depth.

blind spot
The small region at the back of the eye where the optic nerve joins. It lacks any special light-sensitive cells, so it cannot register an image.

color blindness
The reduced ability to tell the difference between different colors, usually red and green.

cones
Light-sensitive cells in the retina of your eyes which detect colors.

convex
Something that is curved outward, such as the lens of your eye.

cornea
The transparent front part of the eye that covers the iris and pupil.

field of view
The amount of a scene your eyes can see at any one point.

focus
The way your eyes view an image to make it clear and sharp.

lateral inhibition
The ability of a neuron (nerve cell) to reduce the activity of neighboring neurons.

lens
A transparent curved disk behind the iris of the eye that focuses light entering the eye onto the retina.

linear perspective
A form of perspective in which parallel lines that recede into the distance appear to converge, giving the illusion of depth and distance.

microsaccades (micro-sacc-ades)
Small, jerky movements made by your eyes.

neurons
The technical term for nerve cells — specialized cells in the body that transmit signals in the nervous system.

optic nerve
The large bundles of nerve fibers that carry signals from your eyes to your brain.

parallax
The apparent difference in the position of an object when viewed from two different points.

photoreceptor cells
Light-sensitive cells, such as rods or cones, found in the retina of the eye.

proprioception (pro-pri-o-cep-tion)
The sense that allows you to keep track of where all the neighboring parts of your body are at any given time.

prosopagnosia (pros-o-pag-no-sia)
A reduced ability to recognize faces, also known as "face blindness."

pupil
The circular opening (aperture) at the front of the eye that lets in light.

retina
The layer of light-sensitive cells that cover the back of the eye.

rods
Light-sensitive cells in the retinas of your eyes which give you vision in low-light conditions.

stereogram
A two-dimensional image that can convey three-dimensional depth and perspective when viewed in a certain way.

vanishing point
A point where two parallel lines appear to meet in the distance.

ANSWERS

pp. 6–7 IS SEEING REALLY BELIEVING?

Fish Out of Water Stare at the fish for 45 seconds, then quickly look at the center of the fish bowl. The fish should magically appear!

Color Confusion How many colors did you count? If you counted 7 (red, blue, yellow, green, white, orange, and brown), you'd be wrong. There are in fact 6 different colors: the orange square (in the center of the side of the cube facing you) and the brown square (in the center of the top face of the cube) are exactly the same color.

Cube Count If you look at the drawing straight on you will be able to count 6 cubes. However, turn the book 90 degrees and you should be able to count 7.

Arc Tease The arcs all come from exactly the same size circle.

Spiral or Circles? It may look like the picture is made up of spirals, but the black and white rings are in fact circles. This illusion is known as Fraser's spiral.

p. 13 EYE EYE

Color Blindness Test You should be able to see the number 74.

p. 29 LIGHT & DARK

Adelson Checkerboard The top right image proves that the two squares of the checkerboard are exactly the same shade of gray.

p. 43 IN THE DISTANCE

Beuchet Chair Check the picture (center right) to see how this clever illusion is achieved.

p. 51 AMBIGUOUS IMAGES

What Do You See? (clockwise from top right) Old/young woman; polar bear/seal; vase/two people in profile; rabbit/bird.

p. 61 STEREOGRAMS

The penguins on the right are the "hidden image" in the stereogram.

Adelson Checkerboard

Beuchet Chair

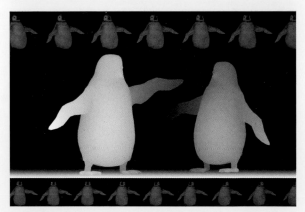

Stereogram hidden image

INDEX